The Sermon on the Mount

The
Sermon
on the
Mount

BY EDUARD THURNEYSEN

TRANSLATED BY WILLIAM CHILDS ROBINSON, SR.
WITH JAMES M. ROBINSON

WIPF & STOCK · Eugene, Oregon

A translation of *Die Bergpredigt* (fifth revised edition) by
Eduard Thurneysen, number 105 of *Theologische Existenz
Heute,* published by Chr. Kaiser Verlag, Munich, 1963.

Unless otherwise indicated, Scripture quotations are translated from the German.

Wipf and Stock Publishers
199 W 8th Ave, Suite 3
Eugene, OR 97401

The Sermon on the Mount
By Thurneysen, Eduard and Robinson, William Childs, Sr.
Copyright©1964 by Thurneysen, Eduard
ISBN 13: 978-1-60899-575-2
Publication date 6/10/2010
Previously published by John Knox Press, 1964

CONTENTS

Translator's Preface   5

Preface to the Revised Edition   11

I.   The Christological Interpretation   17

II.   Jesus the Bringer of the Kingdom   29

III. Jesus the Fulfiller of the Law   43

IV. Obedience on the Basis of Grace   65

Notes   79

TRANSLATOR'S PREFACE

The essential concern of this volume is the true understanding of the Sermon on the Mount. It takes the form of a theological exegesis by that person who has played the self-effacing role as the silent partner in developing the Theology of the Word. In the Preface to the second edition of his *Romans*, Karl Barth said it was "especially the suggestions of Eduard Thurneysen that had seemed to me sound." Barth goes on to say that Thurneysen "read and criticized the whole manuscript as it was being prepared. By inserting many corollaries that deepened, explained and sharpened, insertions I have usually adopted without alteration, he erected for himself a hidden monument in a very selfless way. No specialist will figure out where in this tried and tested teamwork the one began and the other left off."[1] In the volume honoring Thurneysen on his seventieth birthday Barth denied "that I was the active partner who did the giving and Thurneysen only the passive or receiving one."

> On the contrary he was the one who first put me on the trail of Blumhardt and Kutter and then also of Dostoevsky, without whose discovery I would not have been able to write either the first or the second draft of the commentary of Romans, but instead —who knows?—I might actually have embarked

on the attractive career of an Aargau trade-union man and councillor. Also during my time in Göttingen the correspondence and exchange of thought with him was more necessary to me than daily bread: not just because I knew how he enjoyed my tales and because I could confide to him as to no other person my constantly increasing rather than decreasing cares and troubles, not just because he represented the most living bond between me and the distant but unforgotten homeland, but because there was in me constantly the deepest need to hear his judgment concerning my behavior and, while I followed my star as he followed his, to take my bearings ever afresh in relation to him, since I had to understand him and be understood by him in order to understand myself aright.[2]

In 1927 Thurneysen became pastor in Basel where he was the leading preacher at the cathedral throughout Basel's whole Barthian period. Since 1930 he has also been Professor of Practical Theology at the university there.

The distinctive trait of Thurneysen's interpretation is his insistence that the Gospels be read in the light of the gospel and that the Sermon on the Mount be interpreted integrally in terms of the Gospel in which it stands and as well as of the whole Bible, i.e., in terms of the revelation of the grace of God in Jesus Christ.

This distinctive interpretation of the Sermon on the Mount stands in rapport with a series of emphases in the modern study of the Sermon on the Mount. Only a few years earlier James Moffatt had called attention to the great word of grace with which the Sermon on the Mount opens:

> When Jesus promised, "Blessed are the poor in spirit, for theirs is the Kingdom of heaven," his grace-word implied that full provision was made for those who felt beggars before God, instead of feeling self-satisfied and in need of little or nothing. He sees no future for those who rest on their own resources. It is those who are conscious of incapacity to help themselves or to nourish their "spirits," it is they to whom God's bliss is promised. Paul declares that the Lord provided what he promised. He put men in the way of becoming rich in faith and hope. By his self-sacrifice, he brought within reach of humble, believing folk an experience of God and life such as otherwise they could not have possessed.[3]

Whereas the blessing upon those with "righteousness" in Matthew 5:6 would sound to the Greek ear like a blessing upon the morally upright, the Semitic ear would hear "righteousness" as "vindication," "deliverance," "salvation." Or, as Rudolf Bultmann expresses it: "By those who 'hunger and thirst after righteousness,' Matthew 5:6 obviously does not mean those who, 'ever striving, endeavor' to attain ethical perfection, but those who long to have God pronounce the verdict 'righteous' as his decision over them in the judgment."[4] The Sermon on the Mount opens with the blessing upon those who hunger and thirst after righteousness, for they shall be filled with a righteousness that exceeds the righteousness of the scribes and Pharisees. Those who come to our

Lord Jesus Christ shall never hunger, those who believe
on him shall never thirst! Hence Ernst Fuchs can speak
of "Jesus' witness to himself in Matthew 5."[5]

In a lecture at St. Andrews in the summer of 1955,[6]
Joachim Jeremias, to whom Thurneysen refers in his Preface, points out that Jesus and Paul had the same con-
flict with the self-righteous and arrived at materially the
same position:

> Nowhere is the connection between Paul and Jesus
> so clear as here. The Pauline doctrine of justification
> has its origin in the conflict with Judaism, i.e., with
> the attempt to save oneself. The same conflict ap-
> pears in the conflict of Jesus with the Pharisees in
> regard to their religious self-righteousness. Both
> Jesus and Paul are sure that nobody is so far from
> God as the self-righteous person. The Pauline doc-
> trine of justification is the development of the
> preaching of salvation by our Lord: "Blessed are
> the poor" (Matthew 5:3); "I am not come to call
> the righteous, but sinners" (Matthew 9:13); it is
> also the central message of his parables.[7] This is the
> character of God. He is the God of the poor and
> needy, of the despairing and them who have no
> merit. Both Jesus and Paul proclaim God's great
> gift. Jesus says: "The beggars before God are
> blessed"; Paul says: "The ungodly ones are justi-
> fied." It is the same message, only the terms are
> changed.

This interpretation of the Sermon on the Mount was
that of the Protestant Reformers. The Beatitudes are the
Gospel Lesson for All Saints' Day—the day when Luther

nailed the ninety-five theses to the door of the church
in Wittenberg, the day when Cop delivered his Rectoral
Address, the address Calvin had co-authored, to the University of Paris. The Larger Catechism of the Westminster
Assembly, in its exposition of the fifth petition of the
Lord's Prayer, which is an integral part of the Sermon
on the Mount, gave official status to the interpretation of
the Sermon on the Mount in terms of the Gospel:

> In the fifth petition (which is, *Forgive us our debts,
> as we forgive our debtors*), acknowledging that we
> and all others are guilty both of original and actual
> sin, and thereby become debtors to the justice of
> God, and that neither we nor any other creature
> can make the least satisfaction for that debt: we
> pray for ourselves and others, that God of his free
> grace would, through the obedience and satisfac-
> tion of Christ apprehended and applied by faith,
> acquit us both from the guilt and punishment of
> sin, accept us in his Beloved, continue his favor and
> grace to us, pardon our daily failings, and fill us
> with peace and joy, in giving us daily more and
> more assurance of forgiveness; which we are the
> rather emboldened to ask, and encouraged to ex-
> pect, when we have this testimony in ourselves, that
> we from the heart forgive others their offenses.

W. C. R., Sr.

PREFACE
TO THE REVISED EDITION

This little book on the Sermon on the Mount first appeared in 1936. Since there has been a constant demand for it while it was out of print, a new edition seems justified. After examining all the criticisms raised in reviews against the view it advocates and after surveying the exegetical and systematic studies on the Sermon on the Mount that have appeared since its initial publication,[1] I do not feel compelled to undertake a completely new revision. The thesis here advocated, that the Sermon on the Mount is to be understood *christologically*, has gained wide acceptance in the course of recent exegetical work, and yet it must be again and again considered and worked out.

I cite Joachim Jeremias as an example. In his pamphlet on the Sermon on the Mount[2] he investigates the question of the meaning of the Sermon on the Mount. Here he distinguishes three interpretations, one in terms of perfectionism, one in terms of pedagogical training toward salvation, one in terms of interim ethics. He confronts all three views with the criticism that in the long run they all interpret the Sermon on the Mount legalistically. He himself wishes to interpret it as a collection of Jesus' sayings that presents a sort of primitive Christian catechism. The decisive criterion for understanding it resides in the fact that "something precedes" these sayings of Jesus, namely the gospel of the coming kingdom. He writes: "What Jesus says in the sayings collected in the Sermon on the Mount are symptoms, signs, and examples of what it means when God's reign breaks into this world, which still stands under sin, death, and devil." Jesus' sayings "picture faith as it is lived."[3]

I can accept this understanding of the Sermon on the Mount completely. But does not the kerygma that according to Jeremias stands behind and emerges in the Sermon on the Mount, the kerygma of God's reign established by Jesus, call for a presentation of the Sermon on the Mount that brings to light its christological and eschatological content as such? It is with this that the present book has to do. Not only in its Beatitudes, but in all its sayings the Sermon on the Mount speaks of the "blessedness" of the dawning kingdom. In no sense of the term does it have to do with a *nova lex*, not even in the sense of a model that Jesus would place before our eyes for our imitation. Rather it has to do with laying hold of us and of our whole life, so that when we are laid hold of we are placed already under God's reign in Jesus. He who speaks the sayings we find in the Sermon on the Mount is the Lord of this kingdom marching toward the completion of his work on the cross and in the resurrection. The post-Easter congregation in whose midst the sayings of the Sermon on the Mount were written, read, and heard as a "catechism," as Jeremias puts it, had always heard in them God's Christ, risen from the dead and exalted, living in the Spirit and present among them.

In interpreting the Sermon on the Mount in the context of the congregation of today, the point is that those who let these sayings speak to them are to be touched and arrested by them. This occurs in such a way that he himself who speaks is known by us, draws us into the encounter with himself, and thus takes us with him on his new path of the humanity that is in the dawn of the coming kingdom. "The royal man," as Karl Barth puts it, is speaking here—he who in his humiliation let this new humanity dawn among us. Thus he who stands before us here as the proclaimer of the new way becomes himself what is proclaimed. All his sayings witness to him and have in him their goal. He becomes here the "light of the world" and makes us, as his, children of light who put his light on a stand so that it gives light to all in the house (Matt. 5:15).

The Jesus of the Sermon on the Mount, no less than the Jesus who performs miracles, is no mere thinker or teacher. Rather he is a doer, through and through. The complete transformation of our life that is presented to us as his kerygma is the deed of his whole life, which was completed on the cross and emerged into light victoriously on Easter. Like all the sayings and deeds of Jesus, the Sermon on the Mount puts us into the great history of him who opens the doors of all prisons on earth and leads into the open air, in order to "draw all men to himself." What is here proclaimed should do more than inaugurate the monologue with ourselves that leads to an illumining of our existence in a new self-understanding. The sayings of the Sermon on the Mount, like all sayings of Jesus, are to be understood as dialogue, i.e., as an obligating and liberating word of address from him who wishes to come to expression in them, in order that we should become those who answer to him with our whole life.

One cannot really hear and understand aright a single saying of the Sermon on the Mount if one ignores even for a moment the person here speaking. With his mighty, sovereign "But I say to you . . . ," he reveals himself as the Messiah of Israel, the Christ of God. The Sermon on the Mount is kingdom preaching. It raises all the questions of our life, in that it answers them. From this answer our living is put in question, turned around, and renewed. To understand the Sermon on the Mount as a call to "discipleship," as Bonhoeffer expressed it, means to be willing to have our living put in question—as the great liberation from all bonds, by the bringer of the kingdom. He fought for and won that free space that opens itself already here on earth (and not only in a beyond behind the dark wall of sin and death), and he lets us "come behind him" into this new freedom. *That* is what discipleship means. In Jesus, heaven triumphed on earth. The new world took roots in the old world. That is what the Sermon on the Mount is talking about.

No one will be able to say that such an interpretation of the Sermon on the Mount does not do full justice to the concrete obedience of real discipleship. To be sure, such an interpretation (and only it) has put aside a legalistic desire to fulfill the Sermon's commands. Each saying of the Sermon on the Mount calls to us as to a person lame because of sin and death: "Arise and walk!" If, as Jeremias rightly says, forgiveness of sins is really the one thing behind the Sermon on the Mount, then its commanding word is constantly accompanied by forgiveness, as the power of a new life for him who submits to its command. Understood this way, the Sermon on the Mount is gospel and nothing but gospel. Let me repeat it again: "Its sayings picture faith as it is lived" (Joachim Jeremias). They not only picture it, they awaken it. And here "living" and "believing," "believing" and "living," are of equal weight and thus merge into one.

Eduard Thurneysen
Basel, February 1963.

I *The Christological Interpretation*

Like the whole Gospel, the Sermon on the Mount must be interpreted in a way that is basically christological. He who interprets it in other ways misses what it has to say.

We begin with a simple observation. What is the Sermon on the Mount? A section out of the Gospel according to Matthew. And if we face the question as to how we are to interpret it, then the first answer must run: We are to read and understand it from the point of view and in the context of the Gospel in which it is found.

But what does that mean? Adolf Schlatter says: "It is right and fitting that we insist upon reading the Gospel first of all with reference to Jesus. For it was written on his account."[1] He means that the intention of the Evangelist was in any case no other than to open up an encounter with Jesus. He, Jesus, he himself and he alone, his glory, as the fourth Gospel says, should confront us. Who Jesus is, what he does, is in Matthew's own intention the single content, the whole content, of the Gospel. And indeed no one will seriously contest this. But not to contest it is one thing, and it is another thing really to orient oneself accordingly, to desire in a methodical way to hear nothing other than what the Evangelist in his real intention wishes to say to us.

Let us look at the Sermon on the Mount! If what we
have said is true, that Jesus, Jesus himself and he alone,
is the real content of the gospel, then this Jesus and he
alone is also the whole content of the Sermon on the
Mount, since it too is part of this Gospel that revolves
around Jesus. Then the preacher of the Sermon on the
Mount *is* the Sermon on the Mount. This means then that
the Sermon on the Mount only contains sayings that are
intended to be heard not only as spoken by him, but also
—and indeed exclusively—spoken about him. In that
case none of its sayings may be detached even for a
moment from him. As Matthew sees him, Jesus may in no
way be removed from his sayings. He would have to be
thought of in connection with each of them. For he himself would then be the true content of all his sayings.

There can be no doubt but that Matthew himself
wishes the Sermon on the Mount to be understood in this
way. Even in those places where Jesus is not at all speaking of himself, Matthew still has him speak only for the
sake of having him stand before his hearers. I am of the
opinion that we will do well to read the Sermon on the
Mount as the Evangelist unquestionably intends it to
be read. That is the meaning of my first thesis: The only
possible understanding of the Sermon on the Mount is
the christological understanding.

We stand here in opposition to the customary interpretation of the Sermon on the Mount. For one cannot
say that the average interpretation of the Sermon on the
Mount accepted today moves along the lines of this understanding. According to the average interpretation, the
Sermon on the Mount does not at all have to do with
Jesus and only with Jesus in the exclusive way that was

just demanded. Rather this current view holds that Jesus
himself treats a whole series of subjects in the Sermon
on the Mount, subjects which become the topic in and of
themselves, so that each topic can be discussed even
apart from the preacher of the Sermon on the Mount.
The view prevails that in the Sermon on the Mount we
merely have the opinions (of course normative) that Jesus
of Nazareth held in his day on these various subjects
and themes. As his opinions, they are of course subject
to evaluation in terms of our own views on these matters,
views that perhaps diverge widely from Jesus.

In 5:21-48, for example, the Sermon on the Mount dis-
cusses, in connection with commandments of the Old
Testament, the sanctity of life (5:21-26), the sanctity of
marriage (5:27-32), the sanctity of truth (5:33-37), the
sanctity of law (5:38-42), the sanctity of community (5:
43-48), i.e., five important bases of human life. Now the
Sermon on the Mount itself does not present these five
subjects in their independent significance, but rather as
examples to express and document what Jesus called the
fulfillment of the law (5:17-20). Jesus' own fulfillment
of the law, what he has done and does to fulfill the law
and the prophets, is what is involved in these five examples, according to the Sermon on the Mount itself.

Now if one ignores even for a moment the fundamental
relationship existing between these examples and Jesus
himself, then the inevitable occurs: They are detached
from Jesus and become important in themselves. They
cease to point to Jesus and his fulfillment, and they become independent themes. What Jesus said concerning
them becomes a mere opinion of Jesus, such as he might
have had on a given topic at some time or the other. The

interpreter then asks what the Sermon on the Mount says at this place, not about Jesus but about some of the problems of life that one assumes Jesus merely raised. Of course one can say that Jesus' judgment on such problems of life becomes visible in this way. But one may not overlook the fact that this judgment of his, as important as it may be for us, still only serves to point to him, the Judge himself. Jesus lets his light shine. This light of his becomes visible in the illumination cast upon human life with its problems. But it is a discussion of him, the Light himself who wishes to shine here, rather than a matter of the illumination. Of course it must be said that this light can only be recognized in the illumination radiating from him. I repeat: This is what is meant when we call for the christological interpretation of the Sermon on the Mount.

When we scan the interpretive and exegetical attempts to which the Sermon on the Mount has been subjected up to the present, three groups of interpreters can be identified.

The first group to be mentioned is the modern historical school. The best orientation with regard to them is the book by Hans Windisch: *The Meaning of the Sermon on the Mount*.[2] One must say that it stands in fundamental opposition to the attempt to reach a christological interpretation. It explains the Sermon on the Mount fundamentally and exclusively in terms of the history of those times. It does this in a double way.

One finds in the Sermon on the Mount the opposition that exists between Jesus and the theology of the Pharisees in his day. In this view Jesus is the new giver of the law who breaks down and renews the Jewish legal system by means of his purer, deeper understanding of the law of God. The Sermon on the Mount is then "the teaching of Jesus about the better righteousness. It is determined throughout by opposition to the teaching of the Pharisaic scribes. It is better than their righteousness that the righteousness of the Apostles ought to be."[3]

One can well say that this is the dominant view. What is suspect about it is not that the texts are understood in terms of the way of thinking and speaking current at that time. On the contrary that is a service.[4] But what is suspect is the pervasive basic limitation of the interpretation of the Sermon on the Mount to the explanation of the text and words in terms of contemporary material, which is of course remarkably illuminating for philological and historical understanding. To be sure it becomes clear in the process how powerful Jesus' move transcends the Jewish interpretation of the law. Indeed, Jesus bursts open the whole Jewish legal system. But that is not at all the real consideration. Rather the important thing is the knowledge of the person of Jesus himself given with it. In this discussion, he presents himself to us not only as a new teacher of the law who is very sharply critical of the law and distinguishes himself from "the men of old" (cf. 5:21, 27, 33, 38, 43), but also and primarily as the messianic Lord of the law as a whole.

This becomes quite clear in another passage found in Matthew, and which can only be understood in this sense, i.e., messianically. This is the pericope, about plucking ears of grain on the Sabbath, 12:1-8. Verse 8 states expressly that the Son of man is the Lord of the Sabbath. That means, however, that the important thing is not the degree of distance between the teaching of the scribes and the teaching of Jesus. The important thing is only the christological meaning and reference in the statements of Jesus about the law. One would have to formulate as follows the statement by Bornhäuser cited above: The Sermon on the Mount is determined throughout by the christological claim which Jesus raised over against the scribes as he interpreted the law. Then Bornhäuser's statement would be really correct.

The other possibility of understanding the Sermon on the Mount in terms of the history of the times is to understand it in terms of the eschatology of that day. Jesus proclaimed the near end of this world age. The question arises as to how the disciple who hears him is to arrange his life in what is left of this world age. One will live quite differently if one lives believing in this imminent end of all time. One will live only as a person standing under an overhanging wall that at any moment can come crashing down. One will live as a dying man who knows that his days are numbered. The Sermon on the Mount answers this question. It contains the rules of life for those who live in the last days, awaiting the kingdom that is drawing near. As representative exponents of this construction, Albert Schweitzer and Johannes Weiss are especially to be mentioned.[5]

There is again no question but that this eschatological view has valid and well-grounded justification in terms of the history of those times. But it is not important in itself and as such. What is important in it is only its messianic content and reference. This means that even the assertion of the passing away of this world in the New Testament is essentially a christological affirmation. The eschatology of the New Testament is never concerned to make merely an ideological statement about the brief duration left to this age, a statement that as such would have importance and significance, and of which a rather free, speculative use would be made. Instead, this affirmation is important and full of significance only in view of him who in fact makes it in the New Testament, i.e., in view of Jesus the Christ. It is to be understood only as an affirmation predicated of him. He, Jesus, is not merely some Rabbi who teaches this and that, for example, that the world age will soon be at an end. Rather, as truly as he teaches this, he teaches it only to affirm of himself that when the end comes it will come through him, i.e., he teaches it to say of himself that he, Jesus of Nazareth, is the Lord of the end-time.

In the Gospels, Jesus is not the bearer of a teaching of the imminence of the end that could also be thought about and criticized apart from him. Instead, he will bring an end to time when he comes from heaven and sets up the kingdom of God on earth. For he is the Son of the Father from above (cf. 11:20-27)—which is the meaning of all the eschatological statements in the New Testament. The interpretation in terms of the history of the times does not understand this ultimately christological meaning of New Testament eschatology, but rather explains the eschatological passages in a fundamentally unchristological way. The messianic claim of Jesus is probably seen, but it becomes a bare and, as Albert Schweitzer said, "worn-out" idea of the "historical Jesus," who is constructed by this interpretation in terms of the history of the times.

In reality the interpretation in terms of the history of the times, together with this construction of the so-called historical Jesus, cuts itself off from the texts. For this construction is unquestionably foreign to them. They are written as witnesses, as form-critical investigation has again shown, to the fact that Jesus is the Christ. But it is precisely this sole and essential content of all the texts of the New Testament that is given up by the so-called interpretation in terms of the history of the times. It makes Jesus a merely historical figure of a history long past and gone.

It is difficult to label the second group of attempts at interpretation that we have to discuss. In more recent times it is probably best represented by the name of Leo Tolstoy. Beyer calls it a "group of fanatics from the earliest times up to the religious socialists of our day."[6] One may give it this name. But no sort of disparaging judgment should be implied by this designation. This group also build chiefly on the understanding of the Sermon on the Mount in terms of the history of the times. Like the historical school they take up the tremendous sharpening of the law that unquestionably lies in the Sermon on the Mount. Like Albert Schweitzer and his school they read the Sermon on the Mount eschatologically. But what is essential for them is that they do not stop with this historical interpretation, but that they relate the Sermon on the Mount thus understood to the situation of today. They take it seriously in a direct way. In no sense do they reject the word contained in the Sermon on the Mount as a worn-out idea. Rather they identify themselves both with the sharpening of the law and with the eschatology at the basis of this sharpening. They see the Sermon on the Mount smoking like a volcano and they realize the crisis as a crisis not only of former times, but also of our present time and culture, the crisis that would take place at once if the volcano that smokes in the Sermon on the Mount really erupted. And it ought to erupt! It ought to come—the crisis! In view of these interpreters the Sermon on the Mount was given not only for understanding the history of the times, but in order that we may make its message in a direct way our own.

This smoking volcano, this crisis breaking in—this has staggered a Tolstoy as he read the Sermon on the Mount.[7] In his way, Friedrich Naumann has seen that fact in the sense of an either-or for our whole culture.[8] The *religious socialism* of all times was and is aware of this. Something of this knowledge of the dynamite that slumbers in the Sermon on the Mount rumbles on, even when it moves in a quite covered way related only to the inner life of the individual's soul, as in the case of Johannes Müller.[9] And that is quite certainly the virtue of these interpreters, which should not be taken from them! They call for the overcoming of the understanding of the Sermon on the Mount merely in terms of the history of the times, and seek to push through to a direct meaning still lying in it.

And yet their procedure with regard to the Sermon on the Mount must also be put in question. For they too do not really break through to the christological understanding. For them too it is not basically a matter of knowing Jesus, but again only of knowing the problems of life raised by Jesus, as Tolstoy is concerned with the problem of marriage or with the problem of nonresistance. To be sure one may raise the question: Have then Jesus and his Sermon on the Mount nothing at all to do with the prob-

lems of human life? Must it not rather be said that the
whole Sermon on the Mount speaks quite exclusively of
nothing else than the situation of human life and the
questions raised by it? To be sure Jesus in the Sermon
on the Mount has to do with this situation and its questions, but the point is that it is Jesus who has to do with
them! All the emphasis, really all the emphasis in this
affirmation, must fall on his name. It is he who has to do
with the situation of human life, *his* light falls on it. That
is just what must be here recognized: When he enters
and speaks, the problems of human life are of course
raised in the most impressive of ways. But for that very
reason it is a matter quite simply and exclusively of him,
of Jesus himself, and only of him. Therefore everything,
everything at all, rests upon our reading the Sermon on
the Mount with eyes directed only to Jesus and not at all
to the problems of life as such. Then these problems will
be set in the right light, too.

That means, however, that we must read the Sermon
on the Mount without that dangerous, even devastating
"and" with which this second group of interpreters basically reads it: Jesus and. . . Jesus and the problem of
war, Jesus and the question of marriage, Jesus and law
or the state, Jesus and the problem of community. But
this again means that we must read the Sermon on the
Mount in an exclusively christological way. Then the
questions of life will certainly not be neglected! Rather
it is only then that they will be raised as burning issues.
They will be recognized in their insolubility. But just so
they point to the solution opening for us in Christ.[10]
There can be no basic objection to Tolstoy and those like
him beyond the criticism that when all is said and done

he has not yet really sought and found Jesus, the Jesus of the Gospel whom he so earnestly sought. But for this reason he has not really found his path, wandering among the problems of modern life, but has perished in the maze, though accompanied by the Sermon on the Mount, although of course a Sermon on the Mount read by him in his way—and here it must surely be said—in a fanatical way!

The third group consists quite simply of the fathers, the fathers of our church. Above all, they are Luther and Calvin. Of them it can and must be said: They read the Sermon on the Mount christologically and only christologically.[11] It is from them we first learned what it means to read the Sermon on the Mount christologically. According to them it must in the first place be read as the word of the Christ living today. (This stands against that interpretation which is exclusively oriented to the history of the times with its construction of a so-called "historical Jesus"!) And because the Sermon on the Mount is this living word of Christ, it must be read as basically a word of grace, i.e., as a word that from the very beginning and as such treats of nothing other than the fulfillment of God's law accomplished for us in Christ. (This stands against the interpretation primarily calling again and again for our own fulfillment, according to the school of Tolstoy and his disciples.) Its only content is the work of Christ, what he has done, does, and will do for us.

Should still a fourth group be mentioned? Then it would be those who, following the footsteps of the fathers, devoted themselves to attempting a christological interpretation of the Sermon on the Mount. We mention

A. Tholuck, the biblicist A. Bengel in his *Gnomon,* the elder Blumhardt in his little book about the Sermon on the Mount. Among the more recent men, we mention especially A. Schlatter in his great exegesis of Matthew,[12] and Karl Barth.[13] Finally we mention the interpretation of the Sermon on the Mount that Dietrich Bonhoeffer presented in his book *The Cost of Discipleship.*[14] One may compare the presentations of Jesus' proclamation in the books on Jesus by Paul Wernle, Rudolf Bultmann, and Günther Bornkamm. Of course these cannot be counted among basically christological interpretations, for their point of departure is the thesis that one may not ascribe a messianic self-consciousness to the so-called "historical Jesus," but only to the so-called "post-Easter" kerygma. Hence, in spite of the great significance to be attached to details of their interpretation, a cloud lies over the landscape of the Sermon on the Mount. The task of a basically christological interpretation of the Sermon on the Mount must again and again break through this cloud.

II *Jesus the Bringer of the Kingdom*

The Christology of the Sermon on the Mount is that it presents Jesus as the bringer of the messianic kingdom with its new righteousness. The way in which this is presented is to portray the conduct of the man who is called to this kingdom.

We start again with a simple observation. Once more it is Adolf Schlatter who points out the fact that Matthew reproduces the word of Jesus in discourse sections which he, Matthew, has collected from the sayings and parables of Jesus.[1] In every case they are separated off from the following narrative section by the concluding formula: "And when Jesus finished these sayings." This formula is found five times: 7:28; 11:1; 13:53; 19:1; 26:1. Thus there are five such discourse sections, of which the first is the so-called Sermon on the Mount. The others are the instructions to the disciples for their mission, the chapter of parables, the discourse which Schlatter calls the discourse on the church, and finally the sections of eschatological discourse. In their content all these discourse sections, like the whole Gospel, stand under a single, all-embracing concept: the concept of the kingdom. The proclamation of the "kingdom of heaven drawing near" is already in 4:17 the all-embracing statement of the contents of the preaching of Jesus.

At decisive points the Sermon on the Mount too contains this concept of the kingdom of heaven—in the Beatitudes in 5:3, 10, and in the great debate with the scribes in 5:17-20 (verses 19 and 20). The word "heaven" standing alone as the designation for the place of this kingdom which is dawning occurs several times in the section 5:21-48; then the term "kingdom" occurs again in the sixth chapter in the Lord's Prayer (6:10); "heaven" occurs alone in the sense mentioned above in the passage about storing up treasures (6:20); and "kingdom" occurs again in the central saying (6:33); finally the Father in heaven is mentioned (7:11), the concept of life as life in the new kingdom (7:14), and the kingdom of heaven again in 7:21. Thus, there can be no doubt but that the Sermon on the Mount is concerned in a quite distinct way to present the nearing, and indeed the breaking into the world, of the mysterious entity called the coming kingdom.

But what is meant by this coming kingdom? And in what way is the Sermon on the Mount concerned with it? It is this which must now be discussed.

The terms "reign," "kingdom," indeed, "the kingdom of God" (as the Evangelist Luke prefers to call it after its King), and "the kingdom of heaven," as Matthew puts it, all mean the following:

1. There is a sphere of power, and one that is certainly heavenly, a sphere of power which is exclusively the sphere of God's power. God himself is proclaimed, and indeed exhaustively, in his being proclaimed as the King who has this heavenly sphere of power around him at his disposal. This means God reigns and is really God. As the Sermon on the Mount itself says at a decisive

place (6:24), he, as this sovereign and alone omnipotent
Lord, is the One beside whom man can serve no other
Lord.

2. This sphere of God's power is distinguished as the
heavenly sphere from all other spheres of power that
there may be between heaven and earth, distinguished
above all from the sphere of power of man in this world.

Of course this does not mean that these other spheres
are not real spheres of power. Ultimately of course they
are impotent over against God's sphere of power. But
for the time being they oppose God's sphere of power
in a very real way. So the breaking in of the coming
kingdom of God begins a battle against these other
spheres of power, whether they be earthly or super-
earthly in nature. Demons and men defend themselves
against the coming kingdom.

In the Sermon on the Mount we stumble upon traces
of this battle. We have in mind the evil one from whom
we are directed to pray for deliverance in the Lord's
Prayer (6:13). And we think of the passage 6:24 where
the second lord is mentioned, the anti-God mammon,
who stands before us in opposition to the one Lord, the
true God. God's kingdom is indeed coming, but it is still
not finally here; it must first establish itself against its
enemies. But this is far from saying that these other
spheres of power do not also belong to the sphere of the
dominion of the heavenly kingdom. They do belong to it.
They have indeed fallen away from the kingdom and
have in sinful fashion made themselves independent.
The suffering of the world in its whole scope derives
from this defection. But it is just because the other
spheres of power, in spite of and within all their sepa-

ratedness, still belong to God's sphere of power, that
God's government must be erected anew in the spheres
of this world and even in the secret spheres of the inter-
mediary powers that lie above and within it.

3. We must expressly add that along with all this a
mighty "Not yet!" is said of the kingdom of heaven. It
has drawn near, but it has not yet really dawned. It is
here, but at present only in that it stands before the
doors of the world. The overthrow of the powers of the
world has not yet finally occurred. It has been determined, it has been proclaimed, it has already occurred
at one place, namely where Jesus cast out demons "by
the finger of God" (Luke 11:20). But all this is only
promise, promise of the real, the final end of these powers.
Neither within nor without is the kingdom of heaven
as such already here. To be sure the Beatitudes say "the
kingdom of heaven is (*estin*) yours" (5:3, 10), but this
"is" is to be understood as a futuristic present, as Zahn
says in his commentary on this passage. That is to say, it
could mean "will be yours" (*estai*). One could also say
that the kingdom of heaven is here, but it is here as
future. As this future which is breaking in, it is here in
the living space of men. Therefore the "is" of the first
and eighth Beatitudes is entirely in place. The fact that
this "is" of the first and eighth Beatitudes is to be understood as a futuristic present is evident from the promises
of the second to the seventh Beatitudes, where only the
future tense occurs. It is of course not really true that the
meek already possess the earth. So long as this world-
time continues, it will never and nowhere be true. But
it will be true when the kingdom comes. Hence as
promise, as assurance, it is now already true, and also

means something already today in this world-time that is still continuing. Precisely as this assurance the kingdom of heaven is now already changing the condition of the world in an impressively real way wherever it is proclaimed, heard, and believed. For by means of the promise our situation here is recognized as temporary, a passing one. And with this there begins for us the downfall of the powers, the twilight of the idols who are still reigning. By means of the promise we learn to understand ourselves as members of a coming world. And that lends us an indelible character, which we cannot lose. We become pilgrims between two worlds. We still belong to this passing world and yet we are already members of the body of Christ's kingdom that is coming.

4. This does not mean at all that the kingdom of God is a static entity. It is dynamic through and through, an entity that is properly understood only where it is seen and—what is decisive—*proclaimed* as in motion, coming, dawning. Because it is not yet here but yet is coming, it must be proclaimed. It dawns in being proclaimed, by awakening men still asleep and thus laying hold of them and moving them, apprehending and moving them in that hidden and yet mighty way described in the great parable chapter, Matthew 13. This proclamation in which God's kingdom dawns is intended and called for in the Sermon on the Mount, in the sayings about the salt and the light and the city set on the hill (5:13-16). This proclamation is necessary and must succeed. Wherever the kingdom of God dawns, witness must be borne to it. This witness is itself the way in which the kingdom dawns on earth.

5. And now a last and concluding statement. It must

be said that this kingdom is certainly not an entity, a something, something neutral, thing-like, fact-like. For it is God's kingdom. It is thus the lordly, sovereign, kingly coming and joining with us, on the part of him for whom the kingdom is named. Hence it is something personal. It appears then in a personal way, and not as a fact or a thing. For it makes its appearance in the form of the Jesus who announces it in the Gospel. In that he is here and proclaims the kingdom, the kingdom itself is here. In him and only in him can it be seen and encountered. It is not that the kingdom had dawned as such, apart from Jesus who brings it. In that case Jesus would be only the first among the men who had seen and hence announced it. Jesus not only discovered the kingdom of God, he creates it. He is its Prophet, but as its Prophet he is at the same time its King. The kingdom of God is nowhere, really nowhere apart from where he, Jesus, enters "among us" (cf. Luke 17:21). Hence to come to the kingdom means to come to Jesus, this and no more, that is to say, it means to be a disciple who harkens to his gospel.

When we now take up these definitions of what the kingdom of God is, and when we relate them to Jesus, as they must be, according to all that has been said, then we may conclude:

a. The coming of the kingdom has to do with the knowledge of God as the Lord, and in *Jesus* this Lord comes into view. Let me recall the story, immediately following the Sermon on the Mount, about the centurion in Capernaum (8:5-13). His faith, acknowledged and confirmed by Jesus, consists of this: He understands Jesus in analogy to his own profession as the representative of God, who like God's officer exercises the right to give orders sovereignly on earth.

b. The coming of the kingdom has to do with opposition between the spheres of God's power and that of this world: It is in *Jesus* that this struggle and opposition bursts out. In him it comes to issue and decision. The place of this issue and decision is, according to the Gospel, the cross. Over the Sermon on the Mount there clearly lies the shadow of the cross, expressly in the eighth Beatitude, which speaks of the cross of those who follow in the discipleship of Christ. It is in *Jesus* that this battle is carried through to the full victory of God's forces over all the forces of the world. The location of this victory is the resurrection. The light of this victory lies no less clearly over the Sermon on the Mount. Think of the unheard-of promises that are expressed in it from the Beatitudes all the way to the concluding parable.

c. The coming of the kingdom has to do with the great "Not yet" of the kingdom of heaven. It is not yet here, and yet it *is* here, though as promise. It is in *Jesus* that this "Not yet" is affirmed, as well as the promise of the final consummation. So much is this given in him that he even appears as the Lord and Judge of the coming world. This is the case in his great assertion, "I say unto you . . ." (5:21-48), and especially in the sayings of 7:22-23, where Jesus himself speaks quite clearly of himself as the Judge before whom men must stand at the coming messianic day of judgment.

d. Lastly, the coming of the kingdom has to do with a dynamic entity that breaks into this world by being proclaimed. It is *Jesus* who proclaims this kingdom drawn near and sends out his disciples with the same message, promising them that their proclamation will be accompanied by the signs and wonders of the coming kingdom. Just as this is the case in the discourse about sending out the disciples, 10:7-8, it is also the case in the Sermon on the Mount itself, in the sayings about the salt of the earth, the light of the world, and the city set on the hill, 5:13-16.

In order to bring all this to its ultimate expression, one would have to speak of what the fourth Gospel calls the incarnation of the Word. For that is exactly the meaning of this concept: In Jesus, God is personal, God himself has come among us, really among *us*. This means that God has laid hold of and accepted our life in order to be among us. He has himself thus stepped into the whole "Not yet" of this world-time. In the midst of this "Not yet" he has erected the sign of his *someday* and *then*, the sign of his coming kingdom. This sign is the life of Jesus. He, Jesus, is this sign. And the sign is as such the beginning of the coming of this kingdom already.

The fourth Gospel is not the first to speak of this. In its way the Sermon on the Mount already speaks of it. For what is the Sermon on the Mount talking about? There is no question but that from the first to the last word it has to do with nothing else than with human life. But how does it talk about it? By presenting this human life in the form into which it will be changed when it comes under the light of the coming kingdom.

It is unmistakably human life from the first to the last word. Already the Beatitudes (5:3-12) put us in the midst of a definite living situation, on the earth among the poor and persecuted who are called unto the kingdom of heaven. One may also recall the five great basic ordinances for life discussed in 5:21-48. One may think of the sixth chapter, where the pious exercises of man and especially of the Jewish man of that time are treated, and where both of the great threats under which our life stands are also uncovered: mammon and anxiety. We may recall the seventh chapter, where conduct toward the other who is not yet called to the kingdom is discussed and where the decision inevitably confronting the man called to the kingdom is put before one's eyes.

And yet, how this life is changed! How different it has become from the way we formerly knew it! How new the form is in which it lies before us! The form and deportment of this life is so new and different that we no longer recognize it as our life. Or who may say that he recognizes himself and his life in the guise of those discussed verse by verse in the Beatitudes? Who is able to say he recognizes himself in the guise of those who observe the five basic ordinances for life presented in 5:21-48 as possible and real? Who is able to say he recognizes himself and his service of God in the new way of serving God that is brought out in the first part of the sixth chapter? Who can say he recognizes himself in those who handle mammon and anxiety in the way called for there?

Something has clearly happened, something has happened with this life of ours! It is still this life, really this life we know, but it is as if apprehended by a strange mighty hand. It is taken up and lived by a person who has indeed become like us and who yet has the power to see this life he shares with us quite otherwise, and not only to see it but also to live it, and by living it to show and interpret this life of ours in a quite different and

new way. Thus this life of ours lived and interpreted by
him becomes one great unique sign of that wholly other
world from which he comes and which he brings into
this life of ours by coming from that world into ours.

That is what the Sermon on the Mount is, this witness
to a coming world, but as such the witness to Jesus and
Jesus alone. For he is the person who lays his hand upon
this life of ours in the Sermon on the Mount and erects
in this way the sign of this coming world.

In the thesis put at the head of this chapter, this is
expressed as follows: The Sermon on the Mount is the
sign of the coming world by portraying the conduct of
the man of this coming world. In speaking of the man
of this coming world I have quite consciously not used
the plural. For here there is initially no plural. The man
of the coming world is one man, the man Jesus Christ
and he alone. Certainly the Sermon on the Mount itself
speaks in the plural. It has to do not only with one, but
with many, basically with all of us. And so the question
arises: Are then we ourselves already the men of this
new world? And now we answer in all confidence and
decidedness with Yes. But that we are this, we—this!—
such a plural is true only from the singular of the one, Jesus, who alone is initially really this. Again we confront
the insight: *Via* Christ, only by Christ, and indeed we can
simply say *via crucis*, only by his cross are we what we
are, children of the kingdom. For his taking up of this
life of ours has led him to the cross. And that certainly
means that to begin with we ourselves are *not* all that,
the new man of the coming kingdom.

Need that be said explicitly to an attentive reader of
the Sermon on the Mount? Confronted with the portrayal

of the new conduct of the new man in the Sermon on the Mount such a reader will be like a man who stands in the Alps before a mountain wall without footholds. His path has ended. And now someone says to him: Up there, a few thousand feet above you, the road continues! So we insist: This life of the new man has been lived once and only once, only in Jesus Christ. We insist: If it is still valid—and it is valid—that this new life, though certainly not our life now, yet will become ours, then only through Jesus Christ! In this way we repeat that the Sermon on the Mount is only rightly taught when it is taught christologically.

The mystery of this "through him," the mystery of this *via crucis* as such, is now to be described. From the fact that a plural is used, the fact that we have to do with a "we," one can infer that it is really our life that was laid hold of here by the mighty hand of Jesus. In the Sermon on the Mount our real human life is really brought out into the great light of the coming kingdom of Jesus and it receives in this light a new form—and this is the sermon's ultimate content. This certainly means that a great promise is erected over this human life of ours. In Jesus Christ something has been done with our life. A crisis lies upon it, but also an incomparable hope. In having to do with the form of the new man, the form of the former life still lived by us is broken down, killed. Yet it is a collapse and death through which an entirely new life appears. The lineaments of this new life are drawn in the Sermon on the Mount into the false and disordered lines of our old, former life that is passing away. This is the way the Sermon on the Mount is to be seen, and when seen this way it is gospel, good news. But the Sermon on

the Mount gives this good news only to those who read
it in terms of Jesus and as pointing to Jesus, to Jesus as
the bringer of the kingdom, the Jesus who is recognized
and proclaimed as the Christ in 16:13-19. It is in order
that the Sermon on the Mount may be really the gospel
for us (and not merely some kind of a law that kills),
that we must hold so fast to the point that it is to be read
christologically.

It is a fact that it certainly cannot be read in terms of
its own text other than as gospel. Only at the price of a
radical violation of its text could it at times be read otherwise. Or how is it to be accounted for that it begins with
the Beatitudes? This must be intended seriously. No
matter how non-emphasized one interprets "Blessed are
. . ." to be, in any case there resides in such words the
assurance of a promise. In the first and eighth Beatitudes
it is explicitly the kingdom of heaven that is promised.
And those to whom these promises apply are called poor
and persecuted due to the fact that their life is lived in
the light of this coming kingdom. It cannot be otherwise:
He who comes into this light, his life is changed so much
that it must come to stand in radical opposition to the
form of this world, the opposition expressed as being
poor in spirit and persecuted, and yet an opposition so
full of promise. For he who is involved as are the men
portrayed here can no longer set his hope on anything
other than the coming kingdom. In that he does that and
must do it, he loses everything on which men otherwise
lean. Thus he is poor in a new spiritual way, and yet, in
this poverty, rich. He is pressed to the wall and can only
count on God showing mercy to him as his righteous
servant. He who counts on this is not put to shame. This
is why he is called blessed.

This being poor and persecuted for the sake of the kingdom of heaven is more closely defined by the second through the seventh Beatitudes. The idea underlying the concept of the poverty wrought by the Spirit of God receives its more precise definition from the following terms, such as "those that weep," of "the meek," etc. And the concept of the kingdom gets its full meaning from the designations of "being comforted," of "inheriting the earth," etc. But all this certainly cannot be understood otherwise than as gospel!

How are we to understand the fact that the kind of life presented in the Beatitudes is called the salt of the earth, the light of the world, a city that is seen from all sides (5:13-16)? How are we to understand this fact if not as gospel? Or is it only an imperative, a command? "Let your light shine before men" (5:16) is explicitly a command, but it is a command giving life, commandment that is full to the brim with *fulfillment* that comes in, with, and under this commandment. This fulfillment is expressly proclaimed in the great pericope which is to be understood as the key to the whole Sermon on the Mount, 5:17-20. Verses 5:21-48 have to do with requirements not only set up in the coming kingdom but also fulfilled by the bringer of this kingdom (5:18). For these verses present the great basic pillars that sustain the life of man: the sacredness of life, of marriage, of truth, of law, of community.

Hence we need to point emphatically to what Karl Barth (in the footsteps of H. F. Kohlbruegge) has rediscovered,[2] that all the "thou shalt" 's and "you should" 's in the Sermon on the Mount may be understood as the future of promise: "you will . . ."! For example, 5:48: "you will be perfect . . ." (literally paraphrased: you will be directed to the goals that are God's goal). Of course one can also translate all these passages "you should," for they are given in the form of commandment, but it is "you should" because you have received the promise of the kingdom of heaven. And this promise points in the direction of affirming that you will be these men called by God's goals and hence directed to and moved by them. Hence the requirements are expressly meant in the sense of "being what you are." This is the way Karl Barth[3] interprets the passage 6:24. Here there is no "thou shalt," but rather a "you cannot": "You cannot serve God and mammon!" To be sure you could still very well do that, in that you are still children of this old passing world— and yet you can no longer do it in that you are called to be members of the new coming kingdom. That is gospel in the form of commandment. And this is the way the whole Sermon on the Mount is to be read.

III *Jesus the Fulfiller of the Law*

The Sermon on the Mount's presentation of the conduct of the new man of the coming kingdom presents the commandment under which the Lord of this kingdom places the whole life of his people. This commandment is that we are to serve him as the one Lord beside whom there is no other. But to the extent that this new man is Jesus Christ himself, this law is totally fulfilled in him. It is as this law fulfilled by himself that he proclaims it to us in the Sermon on the Mount. That the law is valid over us, but also that Christ Jesus is its Fulfiller for us, is the gospel in the law of the Sermon on the Mount.

We are now to treat the question of how and why the gospel appears in the Sermon on the Mount in the form of law. We have in mind that we are the ones really addressed in the Sermon on the Mount—we in the plural. Certainly, it is still basically true that in all it says, the sermon does not deal with us primarily, but rather with Jesus Christ alone. But it speaks of him by his speaking of *our life*. He takes as it were our life in his hands, and now in his hands it attains that new form of which we spoke. He holds this new form of our life before our eyes in the Sermon on the Mount. When that occurs, this new form of our life becomes the commandment for us. It claims us. In being addressed we are commanded—"But I say unto *you* . . . !" "*You* should!" (5:22, 28, 32, 34, 44, 48). It cannot be otherwise. The coming world desires to dawn, dawn among us. It cannot dawn otherwise than by saying to us that our life must become a wholly new life in terms of this coming world.

Ultimately this is the point that all the interpreters of the Sermon on the Mount have had in mind all along. They all speak in one way or another of the Sermon on the Mount as a *law*, the law of the new life that dawns with Christ. Admittedly the expression "law" is not used in this comprehensive sense in the Sermon on the Mount. Only at three places does the term occur (5:17, 18; 7:12). But in all three places the expression "the law and (or) the prophets" is used in the technical sense of the document of the revelation, the Old Testament. Yet there is another expression in the Sermon on the Mount, the expression "righteousness," which means the comprehensive thing we customarily express with the concept of the law. Righteousness means in the Sermon on the Mount the new form of life in terms of the commandment directed to us. It is used in this way in 5:6, 10, 20; 6:1 (r.s.v.: "piety"), 33. Literally understood, righteousness means in these places the right behavior, the right state of human life, and that before God in view of his kingdom coming in Jesus. This rightness of our life as fulfilled in Christ and promised to us and therefore also commanded us is really the whole content of the whole Sermon on the Mount.

Righteousness understood in this way is missing in our present life. But it is to come to us. For it is the one essential, so much so that hunger and thirst for it must emerge in those who have caught sight of it (5:6). For its sake a person will endure persecution (5:10). It is the great crisis of all former, pretended righteousness, of the human righteousness falsely claimed by the scribes (5:20). It forms the whole hidden content of the new action of the new men (6:1). It is the comprehensive, central commandment of the coming kingdom as a whole (6:33). It is already demanded of us in the revelation of the old covenant. From there Jesus took it up and so only renewed what God had already said "to the men of old" (5:21-48). Its content is concretely formulated in 6:24 in dependence upon the first commandment: You can only serve God if you serve him as the one Lord! That gives the meaning of all the requirements of God. They all mean God's total claim upon the whole life.

This is made clear in detail by the explanation of the commandments that takes place in 5:21-48, in the un-heard-of way of erecting the unscalable wall of true obedience to God. It is a matter of the hallowing of life, but so much so that the slightest notion of ill-will toward the neighbor is a breach of the commandment. Then there is the hallowing of marriage, but so much so that even the lustful look is the breach of the commandment. There is the hallowing of truth, but so much so that even the taking of an oath betrays our disobedience. There is the hallowing of law, but so much so that the application of force is disobedience, even when it is for the preservation of law—and precisely then. There is the hallowing of community, but so much so that even the enemy and he most of all must be taken into the community. This is the way God wills to have the law kept in his kingdom. The new perfection promised and com-

manded, commanded and promised to those called to the
kingdom, consists in being completely devoted to this
goal.

But what does this mean? We know the profound up-
heaval which once came upon Tolstoy and, long before
him, upon the fanatics of the period of the Reformation,
and which even now comes upon every honest hearer of
the Sermon on the Mount. Not without reason! For there
is really erected before us that mile-high wall which we
cannot master. But now everything is focused on the
question: Ought we, must we nonetheless try to climb
it? Speaking non-figuratively, must and should we read
and hear and listen to the Sermon on the Mount as law
and only as law, i.e., as a law that we have to fulfill? Or
do we realize that, as the law which it in fact is, the
Sermon on the Mount proclaims nothing else, really
nothing else than Jesus Christ, Jesus Christ alone?

But what does that mean? It means that the question is
whether we see or do not see that the law of the Sermon
on the Mount is the form in which *the gospel* comes to us
here. If we see this, then the law speaking to us here will
become for us a law that does not kill but rather calls us
to life. For in all its sayings it describes nothing else than
life, that life which is right before God. Of course it is a
life that has never and nowhere been attained, begotten
or created by man, for we men do not fulfill the law of
this life. And yet it is a life that comes to us from Jesus
Christ who alone has fulfilled the law of this life. The
coming of this life to us from Christ is grace, and seeing
and accepting it as coming to us as if it were our own
life—and in Jesus Christ it has become our own life—
that is faith. In this way our life becomes right before

God from grace through faith. That is the gospel in the law of the Sermon on the Mount.

It is no coincidence that at this decisive place we have grasped the central words of the gospel of Paul. He understood Jesus in these words: "from grace through faith," and he did it precisely in struggling with the law. It is not a coincidence that we also find the other word in Paul, the word "righteousness," in which the Sermon on the Mount summarizes the whole law. But again, it is precisely in Paul that we find this word only signifying the righteousness we do not create, but which is reckoned to us in mercy.

Please do not mention that stupid view tolerated all too long within theological research, that Paul has misunderstood Jesus and imported into the simplicity of the synoptic Gospels his own theology. This is truly no interpolation, but rather the only legitimate and authentic apostolic interpretation that the New Testament itself has given to the Sermon on the Mount. Do we wish to understand it in some other way? This nonsensical possibility is permissible. We could read and hear the Sermon on the Mount *without* Jesus as the Christ, *without* reading and hearing in it grace and faith. Then of course what Paul knew full well will immediately happen. The law read only as law, the law read without grace, becomes the law that kills. For it becomes the law that *we* ought to fulfill and can never fulfill. Then the Sermon on the Mount darkens the whole heaven above our lives. The Gospel is silent. The word of Jesus becomes the word of remorseless demand and judgment. Hell opens up before us. There remains only a curse, or despair.

Is it not written in the Sermon on the Mount itself that

we ought to read it quite differently, that is to say, that we ought not to read it without Jesus Christ? It does occur in that section which we would like to designate as the very key to the Sermon on the Mount: 5:17-20. There Jesus speaks of the fulfillment of the law by himself in the Sermon on the Mount itself. It is of supreme importance that this section be rightly understood. The word "fulfilled" (*plerosai*) is constantly understood by interpreters in a false way, and emptied of its own proper content, as though it were only intended to affirm the platitude that Jesus has in mind merely a certain sharpening and amplification of the Old Testament law. Such a view tacitly presupposes the possibility of our human fulfillment not only of the Old Testament law but also of the New Testament law sharpened by Jesus. In fact, however, a glance at the numerous places where "fulfilled" occurs in the same sense[1] proves that it means fulfillment through Christ in the sense of accomplishment. According to his own words Jesus stands before us as the one who has accomplished the law, and that as the bearer of our life, which means in our stead. It is thus that he proclaims the law to us.

This does not exclude, but rather includes the thought that our not fulfilling the law is measured and exposed by his fulfilling. We may think again of the whole following section, 5:21-48. The depth of our sin is uncovered. But it is uncovered by him who, by uncovering it, fills it up, so to speak, through his fulfillment. We are familiar with the Pauline formula, "for us," which expresses this fact. In the Sermon on the Mount the expression does not occur. But the fact itself to which it refers is quite clearly present. We have in mind the word "mercy" (5:7), by means of which the coming kingdom of Christ is made concrete as the kingdom of grace in the promises of the Beatitudes. We may recall the whole section on prayer in the sixth chapter (6:5-15). What is the intention of the invitation to invoke God as our Father, when coming from the Jesus who had just erected the steep wall of commandments before us, if we may not assume that the abyss of our sin is bridged by him—that our separation from God, our not fulfilling his will, is in fact not the last word? What is the particular point of the fifth petition in Jesus' prayer, the petition for forgiveness, if this forgiveness is not proclaimed through him as actually existent for us? We again recall "you cannot . . ." (6:24). What is the point of this "you cannot" addressed to us, if it is not to be a reference to an ability that surely is not created by ourselves, but promised us in this saying of Jesus, an ability to serve God as the one Lord?

Finally we have in mind especially the whole of chapter seven. The series of sayings beginning with 7:1 unquestionably marks a new section. For here the question emerges as to the way in which those whom Christ calls act toward others, first to those outside who have not yet heard the call to the kingdom or who oppose it, but also especially to those in their own number who pervert the call to the kingdom of God and his righteousness (6:33) by hearing the sermon of Jesus, but not in such a way as to do it (7:21, 24, 26). But doing it means here, when confronted with this saying of Jesus, not man fulfilling the law. Rather, in view of Christ's fulfillment of the law (5:17), hearing the word of Jesus aright, hearing it in such a way that in hearing it one becomes its doer (cf. James 1:22), means to place oneself with one's whole life into that fulfillment in Christ. Then one is on the narrow way that leads to life (7:13-14). Then one is the good tree that really brings forth good fruit (7:16-20). But all the "doing" that is done outside of Christ and his new righteousness is lost. No matter how good and great the fruit that had apparently ripened seemed to be—even if a person prophesy and cast out demons (7:22)—Christ still will not recognize such a false doer, but will send him away as an evildoer (7:23).

It is quite clear that no other interpretation is possible: The seventh chapter like the whole Sermon on the Mount has to do with life, man's life, his activity, his doing, but with this life, activity, and doing so that it is based entirely and exclusively upon Christ and him alone with his merciful judgment, i.e., upon grace and grace alone. If a person bases his life here, then he is the man who builds his house upon the rock (7:24-27). It is in this way, i.e., strictly christologically, that the concluding parable of the Sermon on the Mount must be understood. It is certainly not a matter of general moral instruction religiously motivated, but rather of the proclamation of the coming of the kingdom and the new deportment of man. Hence the woes and storms of this concluding parable are not to be understood as merely banal and secular, as the buffetings of fate, such as come with the life of man. Rather what is meant is the messianic woes of judgment breaking in with the coming of the kingdom, the trials to which the hearer of Jesus is sure to be exposed (cf. 5:10-12). He who survives in these woes is he who builds his house upon the rock. The house built upon the sand means the fulfillment of the law by one's own power, as represented by the scribes and the Pharisees of the Jewish Church who are far from the new righteousness of Christ (5:20).

This fulfillment of the law in one's own strength presents, to be sure, a doing, indeed a very lively doing. As the parable puts it, there is the building of a house, a house that is enough like the house built upon the rock to be mistaken for it. The false fulfillment of the law provides the basis for a formation of life, a transformation of life, which really looks impressive when seen from outside. Amazingly wonderful things are cited: prophecies, the casting out of demons, and mighty works (7:22). But in the building of a house the decisive thing is not only the building as such, but rather the foundation. And here the foundation is sand. In spite of all the appeal to Christ, in spite of saying "Lord, Lord" (7:21), the house is still not built upon the word of Christ. Or expressed in still another way: The false fulfillment of the law also leads to the ripening of real fruit. They hang on the tree and are there to be seen, and yet they are deceptive. For the tree is bad, and how could a bad tree bring forth good fruit (7:16-20)? How can a deed not coming from Christ's fulfillment of the law be done in true righteousness?

Here a more detailed word is necessary about the whole context of the passage in question (7:15-23), a passage often misunderstood not only by the popularizers but also by learned interpretation. We begin with 7:21. One usually thinks that these words summarize the exhortations with which the close of the Sermon on the Mount has to do. In this view such a summary would mean that there are those who merely say "Lord, Lord," but do nothing. One cannot merely say it, one must also

do it. Expressed in modern terms: It is the battle against
the merely verbal Christianity practiced by the theolo-
gians in their teaching and their worship, in defense of
a Christianity of action. At least in the practical interpretation of the Sermon on the Mount this opposition plays
again and again a dangerous role.[2]

It is clearly not a matter of this platitude, for 7:22
shows clearly enough that those who say "Lord, Lord"
are not at all do-nothing disciples of Jesus, but rather
display a very active and potent conduct, and thereby
appeal to Jesus. They do various very decisive things.
As we have said, they prophesy and cast out demons. It
is not that they have a doctrine and a cult but lack the
life to go with them. Quite the contrary. They are not
at all lacking in life. What is certainly lacking is doctrine,
to put it in modern terminology. Not their deeds, but
their appeal to Jesus will be rejected "on that day" (7:22).
"Mighty works" they have done (7:22b), and that expressly in the name of Jesus. But Jesus himself knows
nothing of them, he himself as the Judge at the last day
will not acknowledge them. Why not? Is it that a person
would do better not to call upon Jesus at all? Is it wrong
and forbidden to say "Lord, Lord" at all? No one will
seriously maintain that. Why then was not only the
Sermon on the Mount written, but the whole Gospel as
well, if not to arrive at a right confession to Jesus as the
Lord?

But a *right* confession! One can also confess Jesus in
a wrong way. One can be a "false prophet" (7:15). Such
a person can do great things, and yet with all his great
deeds he is still on the way to damnation and not to life
(7:13). He has still built upon the sand. It is not a

matter of setting the doing of good over against a lazy not-doing, nor is it a matter of preferring a discipleship without confession to an empty saying of "Lord, Lord." Rather it is a matter of confession—the right confession over against a false confession. It is a matter of doing, but in the sense of pointing to the roots from which true doing alone can flow. This root is the true confession to Christ. Here teaching and living, confession and life, are not torn asunder, either in exalting the confession above the life or the life above the confession. Rather, confession and life are here revealed in their indissoluble union. In the whole Sermon on the Mount the question has to do with true life. The true confession, the confession to Christ Jesus, generates true life—this is the answer of the whole Sermon on the Mount. Thus in the last analysis the Sermon on the Mount has to do with nothing else than Jesus the Christ.

Materially speaking, this confession to Jesus is the confession to the Lord whose people will "not be judged" by him (7:1), but will "obtain mercy" (5:7) "on that day" (7:22), the messianic day of judgment. He himself will "confess" them as his people in distinction to those who must depart from him (7:23). And this will be salvation for this people of his in the judgment of that day. But he will only do this if his people really hold to him as his people, and this means if they recognize him as the one Lord from whose judgment life or condemnation will really proceed (7:13-14). It is he who decides. This is what his people must know. It is not human doing that decides, and not merely saying "Lord, Lord." *He* decides, for he is really the Lord of the coming kingdom. This is exactly the reason why the promise of this kingdom is so certain, because he is this Lord beside whom there is no other. His decision of grace would not be a decision of grace if there were something else upon which his people could rely or to which they could appeal. There are not even mighty works that may have been done in his name (7:22). He announces himself in his sayings as this Lord of all might and hence of all grace. They all are basically works of grace from this coming Lord, who alone is mighty; that is their complete content.

Only he who hears them thus "hears and does" them (7:24). Whoever hears them otherwise, whoever hears them, e.g., only with some limitation, only in a qualified sense as words of grace, whoever places alongside or against them some deed of his own, a fulfillment of his own—such a person "hears and does not do them" (7:26). He will not stand in the judgment, for the final judgment consists in its becoming clear "on that day" that all lords and lordships alongside of and apart from the one Lord are over. He alone will still be there and reign, he and his kingdom. And the grace in this judgment consists in the promise to his people: The Lord of the kingdom himself wishes to call them away and indeed will call them away from the service of the other foreign lords (6:24), and make them to be that spiritually poor people which with "sound eye" (6:22) looks only to him and seeks the righteousness of his kingdom. Such a people he can accept. The deceitful message of the false prophets (7:15) is that they obscure this view of things from his people, carry them away from this confession to their Lord and point them to something else than to grace alone.

That this whole context (7:15-23) is to be understood

this way is made clear from what is emphasized twice about knowing the true disciples from their fruits (7:16, 20). As the whole context shows, both verses are to be understood eschatologically and hence are to be translated in the future tense: "You will know them by their fruits." This future is to be related to "that day," which is expressly named the messianic day of judgment in 7:22-23 as the final word of the Sermon on the Mount. There and then, in the messianic judgment, one will recognize Jesus' true disciples by their fruit. But that means that here and now, in this time, in the world as it still stands, one cannot know them. Here and now there is only the promise that you will know them. This of course means that there are "fruits," "good works" (5:16); they are expressly promised and commanded, commanded and promised to the person who really hears and accepts the word of Jesus as the word of grace. They are promised and commanded him so surely that they are not dispensable tokens for being called to the kingdom. But they will be cashed in, made unequivocally clear, only at the end itself. Here and now they remain ambiguous to our eyes. Here and now we can only believe that the Lord will look upon and accept our "fruit," our "good works," and that always means our life as lived in obedience to his word, as obedience to his grace. To believe this way and to live this faith is "doing" Jesus' word, for that means to trust in grace.

There is always the temptation to wish to have it otherwise. This takes place when a person thinks he can see and demonstrate fruit in himself or others in direct knowledge, with the result that he will be received by Christ. But, if we may refer once more to 7:22-23, whoever desires this is precisely the "evildoer" (7:23b), or, to paraphrase it, the one who circumvents the true meaning of the law and the prophets, for he circumvents the grace they proclaim. He makes the presumptuous attempt, in assumed obedience to the word of Jesus to whom he too emphatically appeals (7:22), to come before the Judge with a deed this Judge cannot assail. Then he really falls under judgment. Thus it is not permissible, as is commonly done, to derive from this passage the demand: You ought not only to produce good fruit—for that is to be sure demanded—but you ought also to recognize it and make it known as such. No, that is precisely what is excluded here. Good fruit, good works ought to lead to "giving glory to your Father who is in heaven" (5:16). They point to his grace. It is precisely this that is good about them. But just for that reason they cannot be "seen by men" (6:2, 5, 18). For then they would immediately cease to point to God's grace. They would point to something quite other, namely to the man who permitted himself to appear before men with them and who precisely in so doing "has received his reward."

They ought to remain "in secret," that is to say unrecognizable here and now, until God himself makes them known "on that day," until they are rewarded not by men but by him (so 6:4, 6, 18; verse 18, like 7:16, 20, uses the future tense that points to the messianic day). That does not exclude but rather includes the fact that the bearers of this fruit in their hiddenness, in their being known first in the future, already now "let their light shine before men" (5:16). How else could God's grace be praised because of them? It is just by not showing their "good works," in that (according to 6:3 and also 25:37-39) they do not even know themselves as doers of these works, that they are the spiritually poor of the Beatitudes, whose light cannot remain under the bushel. For it is just in this way that they are the bearers and witnesses of that promise which fulfills itself not here but in the coming kingdom. The Sermon on the Mount would be distorted in its whole meaning if our passage were taken to mean a direct knowing and showing of fruits and works. It would then become the preaching of a mere work righteousness, the preaching of religious morality. Jesus would become a mere sage who desires to direct us with God's help to do good. The Sermon on the Mount would then no longer be gospel but only law.

Finally this point of view clarifies everything else that still remains to be read in the seventh chapter.

The chapter begins (7:1-5) with the promise that God's final judgment will pass by those who are called to the kingdom. This promise occurs, in the style of the Sermon on the Mount, as a command, to the effect that in view of this promise all human judgment ought to be avoided. What is this other than gospel, gospel in the form of law? The relation of this passage to 25:31-46, the parable of the last judgment, is obvious. The same proclamation is found there too. Jesus will not judge those who are merciful because of his mercy. Here too the meaning is in no case that we will be spared on account of our works. Rather the clear meaning is that inasmuch as we belong to the recipients of grace called to the kingdom, we will be found to produce fruit which will show on that day that we have received grace. The works are the basis for knowing who received grace, rather than the cause. And what a basis for knowing, itself still hidden, to be revealed only on the day of judgment! Here too it is not moralism that is preached, but rather free grace, and for its sake, as its reflection, human mercy.

Human mercy in view of the promise of the divine mercy is then in 7:2 named the "measure," the only rule of life in terms of which those called to the kingdom have to do with their neighbor. Because mercy is granted to them, they also exercise mercy. Thus they are to act toward their neighbor so as to become witnesses to him of the mercy promised to themselves. Were this rule to be forsaken, if merciless relations and judging were to begin again, then this would immediately involve forsaking the divine mercy. Nothing would really remain but judgment (7:3-5).

In 7:6 is Jesus' warning to the disciples against profaning the word. In Jesus' word, "the Holy" comes to them. For with Jesus' word the divine realm opens up to them. On this rests the whole validity and power of this word, on the fact that it is this holy, divine word. For in that it comes to us as God's word, we are defined as those accepted by God, called to the kingdom. Only where it is spoken and heard as the word calling to the kingdom and emerging from the kingdom, only as the messianic word creating grace, only then does it say and do what it alone can say and do.

There is, however, quite clearly a way of using this word that directs it and accepts it in a different way, so that it ceases to be the messianic and divine word of judgment and of promise. Whoever uses it in this way gives up the Holy. Then it can only produce devastation. That situation emerges which is given drastic expression in the picture of the pearls cast before swine. The result is that it embitters men, instead of effecting their salvation, their redemption. From the context one can interpret this to mean that where Jesus' word falls into the hands of men who understand it again as law and only as law it is profaned irretrievably. For it becomes not the mercy called for in 7:1-5. Rather it works only a fearful judgment. This is what is meant by "casting what is holy before dogs." Compare Philippians 3:2, where this same expression "dogs" is again used of legalists against whom the Apostle must strive in the interest of grace. He who is called to the kingdom hears and uses it quite differently. For with the word of Jesus there dawns for him the kingdom of the God who (as 7:7-11 following 7:6 shows) is a God who exhausts his whole deity in allowing himself to be asked, in order to give good things as he alone can give from his divine fatherhood. So again, judge not (7:1), but, asking, seeking, knocking (7:7), enter in upon the treasure of divine mercy rising before you in Jesus' word.

It is from this point of view that the much-discussed so-called "Golden Rule" is to be understood (7:12). It certainly does not affirm the platitude that we ought to do good to our neighbor in order to experience the same from him. "Whatever you wish that men would do to you" does not mean the wish of the natural man for whom such a platitude could probably still be valid. Certainly what is meant (it cannot be otherwise in the Sermon on the Mount), is the wish of the one who is called to the kingdom. But what can such a one wish from men other than that they meet him with that

measure of mercy cited in 7:2? But this means not as
judgment and law but as witness to the divine judgment
and promises. One looks longingly for such a relationship among men when one has begun to wait for the
kingdom. One "wishes" to have that "from men." One
ought to wish only that! But one will obtain it by oneself
exercising it toward men. For is not the other, in turn,
going to come under the mighty sway of the coming
kingdom if I so meet him that he perceives for himself
the promise of this kingdom through me? So this rule
is a rule, indeed a commandment, but as rule or commandment it is full of good news. It is this apparently
so prosaic word that is a word full of suppressed en-
thusiasm. Not in vain does it contain in itself the fulfillment of "all," simply all that "the law and the prophets"
could promise.

The saying about the hard and the easy way, the
narrow and the wide gate (7:13-14), completes this
whole context. Here everything depends on the content
one gives to the picture. According to the rationalistic,
moralistic, and pietistic tradition, one interprets the saying to mean that the person walking on the hard way
and entering through the narrow gate is simply what one
normally means by "a pious man," the person who keeps
away from all the lusts of the world and by the virtue
of this good work then enters heaven, while the person
on the easy way who enters through the wide gate is
the "man of the world" who follows up all his lusts and
therefore goes to hell. If one follows this interpretation,
then all is lost, the saying is defrauded of its real meaning. For then in place of the new, better righteousness of
the kingdom of heaven there arises the old "righteousness

of the Pharisees and scribes," which is precisely what was to be overcome, since it heads to destruction. Then here at the conclusion of the Sermon on the Mount (in strict opposition to what was said at 5:20!) the law would again be preached in a most threatening way, only as law, the moral and religious conduct of man, commandment without promise. That cannot be what is meant! The saying is a touchstone for the interpretation of the whole Sermon on the Mount, to the extent that it becomes clear here whether the promise is seen in the saying's commandment or not, that is to say whether the interpretation is christological or not. The history of the interpretation of this saying would for this reason be worthy of special investigation. The result would be to show that the false, unmessianic, legalistic understanding far overweighs the right christological understanding. Now the threatening severity, the character of admonition and warning that adheres to this saying, is indeed unmistakable. Here indeed there is command, requirement: "Enter by the narrow gate!" But can the content of this admonition be other than being called to join the people of spiritual poverty, those who sorrow for their sins, the meek who do not try to assert themselves, who instead hunger and thirst after true righteousness, as they are portrayed at the beginning of the Sermon on the Mount? It is they who are meant by those who walk on the hard way and enter through the narrow gate.

But who wishes to reckon himself in this people, who wishes to be found in the way of these who are dependent on the grace of the coming kingdom alone? "Those that find it are few." That is said in a lamenting way quite comparable to the woes handed down alongside the Beatitudes by Luke (6:24-26). Here is uncovered the immeasurable danger in which those stand, who, like the scribes and Pharisees, and with a display of great earnestness and much sacrifice—even appealing to Jesus and goals set up in his name ("did we not do many mighty works in your name?" 7:22)—would like to prance along a religious and moral highway parading a complete attainment.

This very highway could be the easy way and the wide gate that leads to destruction. Why? Because those who walk here no longer belong to the people of the poor to whom the kingdom of heaven is promised. They fulfill the law themselves. For this reason they no longer need the fulfillment by Christ. They think they are well, and can dispense with the physician. But one cannot be sicker than these "well" persons who are unaware of their sickness and hence cannot recognize the Savior who calls them to life. This passage calls one back from this path. But one is not able to hear the threatening seriousness of this call without at the same time hearing the even greater encouragement and comfort here given those who know of their sickness and hence wish only to wait for their Physician and Savior. In waiting this way one is on the narrow way that leads to life, just as surely as he who speaks here is Jesus the Christ.

The parable of the hard and the easy way must be seen together with the two other parables with which the Sermon on the Mount closes: the parable of the two trees, the good and the bad tree, and the parable of the two houses, the one built on rock and the other on sand. The meaning of all three parables resides in what is expressly said in the introduction to the third parable:

"Every one then who hears these words of mine and does them . . ." (7:24). The word of Jesus places one in decision. It is the decision of hearing aright, in which case one "does" the word, or of hearing falsely, in which case one "does not do" the word.

What "doing" means need not be discussed again here. But yet one final thing should be said. This "doing," the doing of the word, is a quite special, qualified doing. It is no work that man could accomplish of himself. Whoever thinks that has not heard the entire Sermon on the Mount aright. Once again everything teeters in the balance. A person can perhaps have heard the whole Sermon on the Mount as gospel, and then at the end understand this hearing itself as a law that man can fulfill of himself. Then one would have stricken the gospel out again and robbed the whole Sermon on the Mount of its meaning. No, the innermost content of these three parables is that man cannot of himself fulfill this commandment itself, the commandment to hear aright. This commandment and precisely it must be first fulfilled for him, in order that he may then become obedient to it. "A sound tree cannot bear evil fruit." One must first be this good tree, in order to bear the good fruit. But no one is originally that. No one begins by being where the Beatitudes are, in the position of those who truly hear, who "do" the word and will enter the kingdom of heaven. If a person does nevertheless—and it is a matter of the opening of closed doors—then it is only because this "hearing and doing" is wrought through the word. The preacher of the Sermon on the Mount calls the "poor in spirit," who are not there; but in that he calls them they are there.

But this means that here at the conclusion of the Sermon on the Mount, as the final mystery lying behind it, *election* becomes visible. One is commanded to build the house upon the rock, to bear good fruit, to choose the hard way. But when it happens it is grace. The Sermon on the Mount is then only understood aright when it is understood in terms of *predestination*. Understood thus it is gospel, since the grace in the commandment of the Sermon on the Mount itself comes to man. For the commandment of the Sermon on the Mount is not only commandment (*Gebot*); it is also offer (*An-Gebot*). For it is the commandment of the Christ who in and with this commandment sets up his kingdom, his lordship over us. The person who recognizes this commandment as Christ's commandment is as such already the chosen child of this kingdom. He is the "every one" meant in 7:24: "Every one then who hears these words of mine and does them . . ." It is thus that all the commandments of the Sermon on the Mount are meant. They all testify to grace, because they all testify to Jesus as the Christ, to the freely calling and choosing Lord of his coming kingdom.

IV   *Obedience*
   on the Basis of Grace

*The gospel of the Sermon on the Mount about the obe-
dience of Christ, who has fulfilled the law for us, does
not exclude but rather includes the demand for our obedience as well. But it is obedience on the basis of grace.
Just for this reason it is real obedience of the real person—and that always means obedience of the disobedient,
the sinful person.*

Now the question recurs in all its urgency as to why,
if gospel and only gospel is intended to be proclaimed
in the Sermon on the Mount, this sermon erects the
mile-high wall of the law before us. Or, to drop the
figure: Why does the Sermon on the Mount present the
gospel in the form of commandments? By raising this
question we raise for the last time the question as to the
meaning of the law in general. And to answer this question we must refer back to all that has been said earlier
concerning the content of the law. The law in the Sermon
on the Mount is nothing other than the description of
life as it is molded under God's reign and government.
Yet the insurmountable loftiness of this law ought to
inform us that it is actually God's reign, *God's* dominion
that is involved. God is the God of whom the Sermon
on the Mount itself declares that heaven is his throne and

the earth his footstool (5:34-35). And this means he is the Lord of all lords, to him belongs all of life, its foreground and its background, and to him it should hence be consecrated. It is not a puny human godling, it is he who is lofty and sublime, whose reign comes here, who assumes again the reins of his kingdom. It is to make this loftiness, this sublimity, this godliness of God impressive to us that the wall of the law (it is *his*, *God's* law!) towers so insurmountably before us.

Yet this is only part of it. The rest is this: It is really man, our human life, which this God, coming to us with his reign, claims for himself. The Sermon on the Mount deals with *this* claiming of us for God's kingdom. By the coming of God's law to us our human life ought to be and will be changed into the new life of which this law testifies. And we have perceived how this transformation of our life into the life of the new man who is wholly and fully God's possession takes place. It is not that we ourselves change our lives, undertaking perhaps to fulfill the law. The law is fulfilled not through us, but for us by Jesus, the Christ, who has come into flesh. The mile-high wall of the law is surmounted by one who has become one of us. We should partake of his fulfillment, the fruit of his obedience. Then at last the high wall of the law terrifies us no more!

Yet precisely so, precisely as law fulfilled by Jesus and only by Jesus, this law remains erected before us as law. And that means we are really claimed. God wills to deal with us. Our life should come into his hand. His, God's will ought to be done in us on earth as in heaven (6:10). He must erect this will of his over us for this purpose alone, the purpose of bringing our life in greater

compassion again to him. That occurs in the commandment of the Sermon on the Mount. And so now it really
means, aimed directly and simply at us: Thou shalt! You
must! Strong, clear, without if or but: Thou shalt! You
must! It is and remains the obedience of Jesus alone that
speaks to us from all the sayings of the Sermon on the
Mount. It is not our obedience. Yet to whatever extent
this obedience speaks to us in our disobedience, to whatever extent he puts himself with his obedience into our
life, to this extent our life is claimed, requisitioned by
his obedience. Hidden in his obedience, our obedience
and our discipleship are called for. The new form of the
godly life sovereignly and majestically fastens its hold
on the distorted form of our tainted life. In our life is
exemplified what God wills and what it means to have
subjected our life to this will of God. By Jesus' speaking
to us we have already come under this will. Therefore
it is no longer merely a law imposed on us from the
outside; it is our own, it is the law of the new life,
insofar as what is here proclaimed has already made its
way among us. Therefore it continues to be true that
we can no longer serve God and at the same time a
strange lord—this "can" to be understood in the un-
heard-of double sense of the duty that is no longer
merely a duty, but is already the being of the new man
in Jesus Christ. It is in this way that we now understand
the commandment of the Sermon on the Mount.

To hear Jesus' word in this way has its consequences!
To become related thus with God is a step heavy with
implications. Yet we are not asked whether we wish to
do it or not. For it is not we who have related ourselves
with God, but God has taken up with us. The decisive

step has been taken. Jesus has taken it from God to us. He has taken it and takes it again and again by directing the word of the Sermon on the Mount toward us. The decisive step reveals itself in that now for the first time we really come with good and legitimate grounds to the question: What ought we to do? Thus we have arrived at the point at which exegesis usually assumes it can begin. One certainly cannot begin here. But one must end here. It would not really be God's kingdom actually coming to us if we did not somehow come to this question, if we did not somehow come to the point that this question tears open, agitates, and transforms our whole life. The "fruits" and "works" required of us mean only such an agitation and transformation as that caused by God's placing this question in this way before us.

How is this to be understood? It is to be understood just as the Heidelberg Catechism is to be understood when it speaks of the law a second time under the title "Of Human Gratitude" in its third part, after it has already spoken of it once. It is to be understood just as it must be understood in the New Testament when, alongside of Romans (and really to be rejected apart from it), there stands the book of James with its requirement of works without which faith is dead. The same is meant in the Pauline Epistles when we are urged to our own obedience in the light of the grand presentation of the obedience of Christ. Embraced within "the mercies of God" the apostle exhorts us in Romans 12:1 to present our life in its entirety as a living sacrifice which is holy and acceptable to God. Our sacrifice in itself is always something imperfect, a bare symbol, that we can perform and that points to the fact that another has accomplished what we shall never complete. This is the way it is with our "works" and "fruits." As we have said, they point to what God the Father himself, and he alone, both is and does for us. They call for praise not for us, but solely for God. It is just so in the Sermon on the Mount (5:16) and also in Romans, where this human sacrifice is termed our only reasonable service (12:1). They are nothing but the reflection of the great light. They are not the light itself, but they cannot be lacking any more than the reflection will be lacking when the light is really shining. The reflection testifies to the light; fruits and works testify to the requisition of our life accomplished in Jesus, so truly are they themselves produced by this requisition.

All this surely does not mean that our life has ceased to be our human (which always means sinful) life. It does however mean that this sinful life of ours is laid hold of by God's word as by a fire that consumes it. It means that in being consumed by the flame of Jesus' word this sinful life of ours itself begins to burn and glow. Or, again dropping the figure: It is not that we fulfill the law; the law is and remains the expression of a life that does not match our life. Indeed, in the presence of the law it becomes clear for the first time how sinful our life is, how completely separated from this other, strange, new life that comes to us in the law. We are and we remain sinners, but we now become, in the coming of the law to us, sinners met and arrested by this law, that is, by the word of our God. And this transforms our life from the ground up. The life of those who are arrested runs differently, quite differently from the

life of those who are still not laid hold of by the fire of
the word of God. We are disobedient persons, but yet
there is an obedience of those who, exposed in their disobedience by God, have become conscientious. This ex-
posure, this conscientiousness is meant by the "purity of
heart" of the sixth Beatitude (5:8). There is this obedience of the sinner, and nothing else is meant by it
than this arresting of the person who up till now has
lived only his own will, the libertine who still has not
been met by the law. There is a "Christian life," a "Christian existence" of the person living here and now, on
this side of the grave, in sin and death. It is the existence
of the person who has been laid hold of inescapably by
the gospel of the coming kingdom and who now waits
in sin and death for the new righteousness of this coming
kingdom, and who while waiting must bear testimony
to this righteousness. This existence, Christian life so
understood, is the final meaning of the Sermon on the
Mount.

What remains to be said is twofold, a No and a Yes.

First the negative. "The Christian life" can never and
in no sense mean that the people addressed by Jesus
were able to do or even merely invited to do what Jesus
himself and he alone did. His, the only absolute purity,
truth and love, fellowship and holiness, remain quite
conclusively unattainable and barred for us as our own
work done by us. He who teaches otherwise, even if
only in the smallest point, will not be called great in the
eyes of Jesus (5:19). It continues to be true that in all
parts of the law, even to the most external and minute
of the commandments, we shall repeatedly have to seek
only Jesus Christ and the fulfillment wrought by him,

otherwise our righteousness will be no better than that of the scribes and Pharisees (5:19-20). For he who might wish to encourage us to fulfill the law of Jesus ourselves would want to bring us to the point of doing it without Jesus and his fulfillment of the law.

If under these circumstances there were still a great deal of talk of Jesus, it would of course only be mention of him to the effect that he stood before us as a model we should imitate. But following Jesus never means imitating Jesus. Following Jesus always means coming under his fulfillment. It ultimately means moving under his cross and resurrection. For there his fulfillment, the realization and the completion of the will of God, is perfect through and in him. Whoever might like to imitate Jesus will bypass the cross and resurrection and precisely thereby commit the real and terrible sin. He will walk on the easy way (7:13). He will dispute against grace. All of this does not remove, but provides the basis for establishing, real discipleship, concrete obedience. There is no dispute against establishing this real obedience. Rather it is precisely a matter of establishing real obedience. But just because it is a matter of this obedience, opposition must be raised against those who speak of it in false, tempting ways. We ought to beware of them as of "false prophets" (7:15). "Beware" not because they speak of obedience, but because they speak of it in that weird way, confusing discipleship with imitation. Their fruits are rotten. Their house will fall!

And now the positive. The situation is that Jesus has fulfilled the law. He has erected the sign of his life's obedience among us. In this way he proclaims and brings us the thing itself to which his obedience points

as a token: the coming reign. We should not think that
we could and would have to erect once again for our
own part this thing erected by him and him alone. But
we should profess this token of his, the token of his
life's cause, the token of his life's obedience. And that
will of necessity mean that the struggle commenced in
his word, the struggle of the coming kingdom of God
against the kingdoms of this world has laid hold of our
own life and now calls for tokens coming from us,
erected by us in our life, as tokens of our being requisitioned by the token of Jesus. These tokens erected by
us consist in words and deeds that are awakened by the
token of Jesus and now for their own part indicate and
testify that God has found us in Jesus. As our tokens,
they are weak and sinful, laden as is everything that
comes from us with the characteristics of our disobedience, but still tokens that speak of that fact that we as
the disobedient are in God's hand. Yes, our life as a
whole will have to become such a token. For it is requisitioned in its entirety whenever Jesus in his word has
laid hold of us. This requisition, and the token demanded
of us that announces it, is what is meant when the
Beatitudes (5:3-11), verse after verse, speak of the deportment of the new man who hopes in God and only
in God. This requisition and the token demanded of us
announcing it are what are meant by the "works" mentioned in 5:16 and the "fruits" in 7:16-21.

The fact that this requisition displays itself in a quite
definite, concrete, evident conduct enjoined upon us—
this fact is the topic for discussion in the conclusion of
each of the five great illustrations in 5:21-48. There we
are told, in the first example, that the person struck by

Jesus' word and awaiting the kingdom of heaven will, when placed under the commandment "Thou shalt not kill," certainly not fulfill this sixth commandment as Jesus fulfilled it. Rather he will give a token of the fact that he knows about this obedience of Jesus and has himself been struck by this obedience of Jesus. And this token demanded of him will consist in the fact that he will no longer flee before this commandment into a false, hypocritical worship of God. Before he goes to the worship of God he will attempt to become reconciled with his enemy, and when he is on the way to court he will do everything in his power to make the court unnecessary (5:23-25). In view of the seventh commandment, "Thou shalt not commit adultery," a commandment which he quite certainly does not fulfill, he certainly will not literally cut away his arm and eye, but he will move toward the erection of very radical tokens, cutting deep into his own flesh, as tokens corresponding in the human, sinful sphere to the claim of Christ to which man can never really attain here, and pointing to the fact that the person who has been met here by the word knows about the purity of Christ, which is not his, man's, but which is the purity of the coming reign promised to man (5:29-30).

Symbolic obedience is demanded when, in view of swearing, the simple truth of every human word is called for (5:37). Symbolic conduct in this sense is meant by the turning of the cheek for the reception of the second blow in the much-quoted verse 5:39, by the giving away of the cloak, by the second mile, and by the loan (5:40-42). Symbolic conduct in the direction of the true community never fulfilled by us but fulfilled in Christ, a fellowship that begins right where our fellowship ends, that is to say, when confronted with our enemy, is demanded by the weighty words about blessing the enemy, about doing more than others (5:44, 47).

Karl Barth once introduced for this symbol the concept "demonstration."[1] This concept, as Barth defines it, can be adopted and used with profit. It means once more that it cannot be our affair to perform, even approximately, the complete obedience of Christ. This obedience stands entirely over against our best symbolic deed, in its own category, as a symbol of the first order, in radical solitude and exclusiveness. Just so, however, this obedience becomes useful for us, a call to life for us, "our" obedience. A demonstration is an action that comes from and points to the entirety of our life laid hold of by this obedience of Jesus, testifies to it, answers and corresponds to it on our human, sinful plane. Such demonstrations are possible and commanded, just because they do not at all wish to be what is impossible for us and what is not commanded, a repetition of the obedience of Christ. In this connection we are also to understand that "demonstration" of which 6:1-18 speaks. This passage concerns the first thing we usually understand by "good works": alms, prayer, fasting. Yet the demonstration that is here enjoined consists, as we have said, precisely in that we ought not to desire at all to "demonstrate" with these good works. We ought to do them, but in complete hiddenness. We ought not to speak of them, we ought not to show them before men. And just so through the complete hiddenness of this kind of "good works," we will do the good work and bear the fruit that is worthy of the coming reign.

Before all else however there belongs here the grand lack of respect demanded in the second part of the sixth chapter, lack of respect toward mammon and toward the spirit of anxiety. We ought to amass no treasures (6: 19-21)! We ought not to be anxious (6:25-34)! We ought not to look through the corners of our eyes toward the powerful who stand behind the treasures and the anxiety (6:22-23)! We *ought* not do it?—no, we *shall* not do it! Why not? Because there is only *one* respect for those who wait for God's reign, respect before the Lord who tolerates no other lords beside him (6:24).

This language is in unheard-of concreteness. The grasp of a powerful hand becomes visible, grasping after the real, daily, sinful life of man. Truly, Jesus is Lord of everyday life! What becomes of us under the grip of this hand? Nothing is sure in his presence, not our gold, but also not our anxiety, not our alms, not our prayers, not our asceticism! Everything must be given up, everything becomes quite new and quite different. There we have again the revolution of the Sermon on the Mount, there we have again the smoking volcano that could erupt any moment! Yes, now some mention may and even must be made of the radicalism of our obedience demanded by the Sermon on the Mount. For now it is absolutely clear: The demand is so radical because he who performs it, in demanding it, is the one who breaks through all bonds, the Victor, the Resurrected. *Spirant resurrectionem,* Bengel says of all sayings and deeds of Jesus, even though they are attested as spoken and done long before the Easter event. They bear witness to *resurrection,* the resurrection of Jesus of Nazareth. Only from there can they be understood and interpreted. The dis-

tinction between a pre-Easter and a post-Easter kerygma
is invalid. The kerygma is one and can be really heard
as addressing us only as this unified message proclaimed
once for all, in its unity and wholeness. It addresses us
in sweeping us into the Easter event as those buried
with Christ in his death and raised with him to new
life. And this applies—to repeat again everything said
before—truly to all the sayings in the Sermon on the
Mount.

What might now follow would be nothing other than
a verse by verse interpretation, in which the general
statement made here would have to be verified. It would
have to be an interpretation that proceeds according to
the rule of the fathers as we have attempted to unfold
it here. Again and again in the church and in theology
the Sermon on the Mount is not read according to this
rule. Rather it is exegeted in a moral or mystical way
(we have in mind, e.g., Johannes Müller), insofar as one
does not prefer to treat it only as a document in the
history of religion and thus to prevent it from expressing
itself at all. Everything depends on overcoming this
moral and mystical interpretation. We say this out of
deep concern over the whole condition of mankind.

We think once again of a word from the Sermon on
the Mount itself. It is the word about the salt that must
be on earth if the life of man is not ultimately to become
quite terribly rotten (5:13). What is meant by this
rottenness? Certainly not merely the moral perverseness
lying all too near, toward whose elimination Jesus would
have busied himself with moral means. Rather what is
meant is an apostasy of a metaphysical sort, apostasy
from the powers and lights of the coming kingdom. What

is meant is a humanity which has been given over to itself in good and bad, which lives without God and without grace, "separated from Christ, alienated from the commonwealth of Israel, and strangers to the covenants of promise," "dead through trespasses and sins," living "in the passions of the flesh" (Eph. 2:1-12). A humanity is meant that includes no people of God, no church of Jesus Christ living among it. The church of Jesus Christ, however, is only that church which no longer goes out to morally elevate the world by its own powers, but which counts only on the richness of God's mercy, "who out of his great love with which he loved us . . . made us alive together with Christ . . . and made us sit with him in the heavenly places in Christ Jesus" (Eph. 2:4-6). This, however, is something quite different, something utterly new. This people, this congregation, this church should and will be awakened among us through the Sermon on the Mount. This can only happen if the word of the Sermon on the Mount, free from all moral or mystical contamination of its interpretation, so speaks to us that Jesus the Christ himself speaks again in his word and lays hold of us.

Since church and theology no longer understand, interpret, and deliver correctly this word given them, the salt fails and the world today is again in the condition of very terrible rottenness. It must be said once again: The church reads Jesus' word given it, it reads the Sermon on the Mount, as law that it attempts to fulfill. That is where this church is no longer salt, nor light, nor a city set on a hill—for this reason and this reason alone! This is why it has so little authority to forgive sins. On the contrary, with its mere Jesus-religion and

Jesus-morality it drives man right into sin. And thus is fulfilled the final parable that Jesus uttered in the Sermon on the Mount! It builds on the sand, and when the storms come—and the storms have come!—it collapses.

To me it is as if I hear passing through the world a tremendous sigh from a thousand voices, from all peoples and lands and races: No longer force us into sin! Do not cast us under the law. Give us, give us finally the gospel! Basically the one same thing is always meant, wherever men, moved by the great shaking of our daily life, complain, quarrel, and cry. The world, yes, the world out there waits for the church to give what the world cannot give: Jesus the Christ in his word. And, thank God, it is not simply not there, it is again and again as by a miracle still there, the true church built by God on the rock. It has not wholly disappeared. It is again today at the task of casting off the bonds of the Babylonian captivity in which it lay bound. We ought also not worry. It is as valid today as it was at first: Jesus speaks. And he speaks "as one who has authority, and not as the scribes" (7:29), and the people, the people of affliction who yet hope in their misery, are astonished and rejoice "at his teaching."

NOTES

TRANSLATOR'S PREFACE

1. *Der Römerbrief* (2nd edition 1922, quoted from 8th reprint, Zollikon-Zürich: Evangelischer Verlag, 1947), pp. vii and xviii. Cf. the English edition, *The Epistle to the Romans,* tr. Edwyn C. Hoskyns (London: Oxford University Press, 1933), pp. 4, 15.

2. *Revolutionary Theology in the Making: Barth-Thurneysen Correspondence, 1914–1925,* tr. James D. Smart (Richmond, Va.: John Knox Press, 1964), p. 72.

3. James Moffatt, *Grace in the New Testament* (New York: Ray Long and Richard R. Smith, Inc., 1932), p. 192.

4. Rudolf Bultmann, *Theology of the New Testament,* tr. Kendrick Grobel (New York: Charles Scribner's Sons), I (1951), p. 273.

5. "Jesu Selbstzeugnis nach Matthäus 5," *Zur Frage nach dem historischen Jesus, Gesammelte Schriften II* (Tübingen: J. C. B. Mohr, 1960), pp. 100–125.

6. Published in *The Expository Times,* LXVI (1954–55), pp. 368–371, esp. p. 369.

7. Jeremias, *ibid.,* points out that the Semitisms in the statement "This man went down to his house justified rather than the other" indicate that the statement, and with it the point of the parable of the Pharisee and the publican, is not due to Pauline influence on Luke, but to Jesus himself, who "was the first to designate the acceptance of the sinner by God as God 'justifying' him (*dikaiousthai*), i.e., as an anticipated eschatological acquittal." Cf. the christological interpretation of the parables by Ernst Fuchs, "Bemerkungen zur Gleichnisauslegung," *Theologische Literaturzeitung,* LXXIX (1954), pp. 345–348, a position supported by Jeremias in *Die Gleichnisse Jesu* (Göttingen: Vandenhoeck und Ruprecht, 6th edition 1962), p. 227. Cf. A. M. Hunter, *Interpreta-*

tion, XIV (1960), p. 185: "Over the whole parable [of the prodigal son], as subtitle, might be inscribed Paul's words, 'God who justifies the ungodly.' This was the heart of Paul's theology, but it was the Lord's before it was Paul's." Cf. Dietrich Bonhoeffer, *The Cost of Discipleship* (New York: Macmillan, revised edition 1959); C. H. Dodd, *Gospel and Law; The Relation of Faith and Ethics in Early Christianity* (New York: Columbia University Press, 1951); and Gottlob Schrenk, in the article on "righteousness" in the *Theologisches Wörterbuch zum Neuen Testament,* ed. Gerhard Kittel (Stuttgart: W. Kohlhammer Verlag), II (1935), pp. 180–229; English tr. J. R. Coates, *Bible Key Words* (New York: Harper and Brothers, 1951).

PREFACE TO THE REVISED EDITION

1. See "Bergpredigt" in *Religion in Geschichte und Gegenwart* (Tübingen: J. C. B. Mohr), 2nd edition, ed. Hermann Gunkel and Leopold Zscharnack, I (1927), pp. 907–913; 3rd edition, ed. Kurt Galling, I (1957), pp. 1047–1054.

2. *Die Bergpredigt* (3rd edition, Stuttgart: Calwer Verlag, 1961).

3. Jeremias, *op. cit.,* pp. 28 f.

CHAPTER I

1. *Der Evangelist Matthäus* (Stuttgart: Calwer Vereinsbuch-handlung, 1929), p. viii.

2. Tr. S. MacLean Gilmour (Philadelphia: Westminster Press, 1951).

3. So Bornhäuser in a programmatic statement in his preface to *Die Bergpredigt, Versuch einer zeitgenössischen Auslegung* (Gütersloh: Bertelsmann, 1923).

4. With regard to this aspect of the matter one must make constant use of *Das Evangelium nach Matthäus erläutert aus Talmud und Midrasch* by Hermann L. Strack and Paul Billerbeck (Munich: C. H. Beck'sche Verlagsbuchhandlung, 1922).

5. Cf. Albert Schweitzer's *The Quest of the Historical Jesus,* 3rd English edition, tr. W. Montgomery (London: A. and C. Black, 1954); Johannes Weiss, *Die Predigt Jesu vom Reiche Gottes* (Göttingen: Vandenhoeck und Ruprecht, 1892, 2nd edition

1900); and Weiss' exegesis of the first three Gospels in *Die Schriften des Neuen Testaments* (Göttingen: Vandenhoeck und Ruprecht, 1907).

6. Cf. H. W. Beyer: *Der Christ und die Bergpredigt nach Luthers Deutung* (Munich: Christian Kaiser Verlag, 1935), p. 7.

7. Cf. Tolstoy, *Short Exposition of the Gospel*, in *The Complete Works of Count Tolstoy*, tr. and ed. Leo Wiener (Boston: D. Estes and Co., 1904–05), Vol. XV, pp. 367–394, and *What Shall We Do Then?*, Vol. XVII, pp. 3–340.

8. Cf. Friedrich Naumann, *Briefe über Religion* (Berlin-Schöneberg: Buchverlag der 'Hilfe,' 13th to 15th Thousand, 1910).

9. Cf. Johannes Müller, *Die Bergpredigt* (Munich: C. H. Beck, 1906).

10. This is an explicit answer to the question as to the contribution of so-called dialectic theology to the treatment of the Sermon on the Mount. The question has been raised explicitly by Johannes Schneider in his book *Der Sinn der Bergpredigt* (Berlin: Furche-Verlag, 1936). Schneider thinks he is obliged to assert that "a really 'dialectic' treatment of the Sermon on the Mount does not exist, surprisingly enough—or should one say characteristically enough!" If Schneider for his part had only recognized more clearly the problem of interpretation posed by the Sermon on the Mount!

11. H. W. Beyer in the book already mentioned has shown this nicely for Luther. Of course one must observe that Beyer places the emphasis much too much and much too one-sidedly upon the doctrine of orders, which to be sure is found in Luther. But for Luther the decisive thing in the interpretation of the Sermon on the Mount is certainly not this doctrine, but rather the fact that Luther, too, understands the Sermon on the Mount exclusively as the divine law fulfilled for us by Jesus Christ. That is to say, he understands it in the sense of the doctrine of justification. That this is not emphasized strongly and clearly is the weakness of the useful book by Beyer.

12. *Der Evangelist Matthäus* (Stuttgart: Calwer Vereinsbuchhandlung, 1929, reprint 1959).

13. *Church Dogmatics* II:2, English edition, eds. G. W. Bromiley and T. F. Torrance (Edinburgh: T. and T. Clark, 1957).

14. Tr. R. H. Fuller (New York: Macmillan Co., 1949).

CHAPTER II

1. *Der Evangelist Matthäus* (Stuttgart: Calwer Vereinsbuch-handlung, 1929), pp. 125 ff.

2. See in this whole context Karl Barth's basic pamphlet *Evangelium und Gesetz*, Heft 50 in the series *Theologische Existenz Heute, neue Folge*, p. 11. Cf. his sermon on Matthew 6:24–34 in *Evangelische Theologie*, 1935, pp. 331 ff.

3. Cf. his sermon on Matthew 6:24–34 cited in the preceding note.

CHAPTER III

1. Cf. Matthew 1:22; 2:15, 17, 23; 4:14; 8:17; 12:17; 13:35; 21:4; 26:54; 27:9.

2. Friedrich Niebergall, *Praktische Auslegung des Neuen Testaments* (Göttingen: Vandenhoeck und Ruprecht, 1909), says on this passage: "Again Jesus' hand falls hard upon the false preference for cultic magical performances, externality rather than simple moral duty. Even the confession of his lordship and deity, even speaking in tongues and preaching, even destroying the kingdom of the world and building up the kingdom of God, do not protect one from judgment, if the simple good is not done. All those cultic and ecclesiastical affairs are not wicked, but neither are they good in themselves; good is only the simple good. It is frightful how soberly moralistic this Jesus is." (!)

CHAPTER IV

1. Cf. *The Epistle to the Romans*, tr. Edwyn C. Hoskyns (London: Oxford University Press, 1933), p. 431.

www.ingramcontent.com/pod-product-compliance
Lightning Source LLC
Chambersburg PA
CBHW071108090426
42737CB00013B/2529